The Magick Of Vanilla Chai Tea With A Pinch Of Damiana

by

Theresa Newbill
&
Kurt Newton

The Magick Of Vanilla Chai Tea With A Pinch Of Damiana

Published by
Hedge Witchery Books
www.hedge-witchery-books.com

Cover image: *Flowering Tea*, as served by 'Flat Caps Coffee', Newcastle Upon-Tyne, England. © Lindsay Caulfield 2011

Chapter One: She Says

I have a craving for Thai food,
it calms me when the moon has
failed to cast its silvery glow and
I find myself deprived of the warmth
of its light.

There are advertisements that blink
like needless little trinkets without
any commitment on their part, even
to hands held out, destitute and most
hardened.

Coffee and pastries just don't do it
for me anymore. I want something
exotic, something that defies explanation
when I close my eyes and recline,
feeling the tang of sweet herbs

in my throat, negotiating their passions
in a preview of coming attractions. If my
body is my temple, then what I put in it can
attract a God, and then it won't matter if I
miss the moon,

or if the sky gradually turns a deep,
luminous blue in the absence of stars,
because I'll already have my backup
plan ready; I will move with him
as one,

like shadows that strike at lightning,
pulling at the forces of the universe
as if nothing out of the ordinary has
happened, barely conscious of anything
other than ourselves;

then we'd vanish into thin air. That's the
love I want realized, where our whereabouts

have no place or geography, and the moon
is silent within our hearts, giving us her
blessing.

~

I think I may have cast a spell. I can feel
him close, like never before. He's smiling,
my twin flame; his legs are crossed, his
face is clean-shaven, and there's an olive-
wood smell that surrounds him.

He's wiggling his nose and drinking from
a porcelain cup. I try not to think about
him, but with every bite of Tod Mun,
dipped in sweet, spicy sauce, I extract
his essence,

swallow it as if I can't get enough. He's
my appetizer of corn fritters and bay shrimp,
that promises me hunger after digestion,
alive in want, craving more, and in those
first moments,

I'm thrown clear off my feet, space bound,
struggling for breath. There's an explosion
of heat as blood spasms with life within me.
Bits and pieces of me fall, dispersed among
the cosmos,

like a script that's fallen from the hands of
God. I watch the second hand of a clock
go round and listen for its click at that crucial
place that keeps me open to the signs; all this
before the noodles and fried rice entrée.

~

Pad Kee Mao- Drunken Noodles, are a clever
way to your tongue. They do exactly what they
are intended to do, manipulate, kidnap your

senses, to a point where you don't give a damn
about atoning for your sins,

because the fresh wild rice noodles, garlic, basil,
green beans, bell peppers, snow peas, tomatoes
and pineapples are enough to want to make you shake
hands with the Devil himself. There are moments
that are just abundant with the flavor of time,

and that have you proceeding, without any choice
in the matter, almost like some sort of conspiracy
to happiness even if in the beginning you find yourself
indifferent to it. My heart can be held on consignment,
but I think about the possible outcomes,

and I understand perfectly that the payment can be
cold to touch, if all of the right ingredients aren't
left to simmer and operate at their own accord. When
it's right; it's like a child warmly eating ice cream
in the middle of a snowstorm.

~

I like the versatility of red curry. I can add any
ingredients to it that I want, from potatoes to peanuts.
Sometimes that kind of freedom helps with the
anxiety of dreams, when you look in the mirror and
the image before you doesn't match,

with what's inside. Today I saw a butterfly outside
my kitchen window, jutting in knife like formation
through the air and I thought about hot cider and the
time my paper bag ripped and I spilled the contents
of my groceries all over the street.

No one helped me pick them up, but from that crosswalk,
I noticed a hand in the air, waving good-bye to another
as she entered a yellow cab. He, didn't wave back, it
was as if he feared waving good-bye to her. Instead
he returned his hands to his pocket,

the same ones that had caressed her face earlier in
the embrace of a kiss, retraced their steps, back to
his car. She wore a wedding ring, from another, yet
without speaking, she said so much about freedom of
love,

when the voices of angels pause for just one brief
second at an intersection, and wait for you to cross
over once the light has change. Red curry burns
bright tonight, and butterflies circle in quick inspection,
before flying away.

~

There's abandonment in the night tonight. When fortunes
are spent and love is absorbed into the atmosphere in
an attempt to heal and engage. Cherubs are our little
helpers and like detached spirits of the dead they coat
our senses and feed our souls with discretion,

touching, silent, like the quizzical frown of a pallet
adjusting to coconut milk broth with tomatoes, cabbage,
galangal, lemongrass and cilantro. It may take us mere
mortals a few minutes to see daylight, but we savor in the
advantages of it when we do.

~

Some people have the ability to restore damaged paintings,
restoration is too neurotic for me; I like the idea of just
being. Imperfection isn't such a bad thing. We can walk
down a crowded street and watch how it works. In retrospect,
our reactions can be appalling.

Some of us don't deal well with vulnerability, with feeling
weak and humiliated, yet there is still imperfection in that
kind of strength, more so I believe. When life has finally
beaten you, is when you begin to live. Imperfection can
be spiritual brethren for the soul.

Today I'm making Ginger Stir Fry, if for no other reason than

I feel like it. We are all true when we dabble into the unknown,
and making Ginger Stir Fry, is un-chartered territory to me. I
suppose that's fitting, sitting silently, hands folded, watching
it sauté, waiting to be interpreted by my taste buds.

~

Kid Rock music goes well with Citrus Apple Snapper. The
combination makes my eardrums and stomach vibrate so
hard for want of them, they hurt. Tonight, I want to want,
to be disappointed, exasperated. I want to play wounded martyr
and to hell with developing a thicker skin.

I'm in a fine mood, I know. But I need to sip beer and fight
off the shiver I feel at being alone with food and music as my only
comfort. I 'd like to wallow in the pain of it all, as I deprive
myself solace, without pity. I'm a walking contradiction, and
I'm not making much sense but who cares?

I don't want to miss his call; I don't want to miss him. Today
I want to miss Kid Rock music and Citrus Apple Snapper. I
want to be cradled and shouted at in the same breath. I want
irrationality. I want to numb by not numbing, let my stomach
churn with rage, my soul empty without music.

I think I'll dye my hair platinum blond and drink more tea.
Tea can be magickal, suggestive. It can penetrate every level
of consciousness when brewed correctly and I'm a witch, I know
about the mixing of herbs. I can dream him up; date him in my mind,
experience him in a field, forged by fire.

~

I'm skeptical about lighting my yuletide tree this year. There's
a fellow writer I know of, but don't know; he wants to collaborate.
I'm afraid at the moment, there are scars he has not seen, that may
leave him silent. I'm met him online only briefly, and we've spoken
like two poker players across the table from one another,

but there's something unsettling about him, about the way he
uses his intelligence, original, with insight and refinement. I

7

think I'll forget about that now, though. He's married with children, and I have Yule to look forward to, and a deceased mother to remember.

~

There's an outdoors café where people with sour faces sip coffee endlessly, talking distantly about worldly things that may or may not affect them. I stumble upon this scene sometime in April, thinking how amazingly fast the season's come and go. I stay comfortable within the changes;

it keeps me from thinking too much, from wishing too much. Everything is fleeting, and options are so limited, I don't know why I always proceed with caution but I do. He's contacted me on and off again, throughout this process of change, that writer on the net, the one who challenges me with every syllable.

We shoulder on one another and talk about our restless conscience. I feel like I can tell him anything, like I want to tell him everything. I'm not an expert on conviction but I know he's a straight shooter, says what he means, means what he says. I try and steer away from false hope,

when I can foresee a scenario ahead like I do with this one. "You're making a grave mistake, you're going to die in his arms," is what I told myself. And those open cafes with the smell of coffee and conversation, who can blame them? There is more at stake now than just the fate of a single man and woman.

~

I see objection as integral part to every love story. You warn yourself, have a sip of coffee, warn yourself again before you psychotically let him back in once again. Sometimes I think it's the coffee. It has me waking up in the middle of the night gazing at his image in my head, turning him on and off,

like a remote control. I look out the window and see the footprints of the morning frost in April, represented so well by lines and squiggles, which match perfectly. I study them; think of him, I study them, think of me,

I study them; think of us gazing comparatively across the scene into Fort Tyrone Park; matching footpaths, perfectly.

~

Today I'm trading in my coffee for Vanilla Chai Tea. Having Cuban heritage it's a bit extreme, I know, but I love the imminent execution of something old as the evidence of something new emerges. There are steady steams of authoritative, proactive images murmuring words in my head,

waiting to be born. Classical music strikes chords at noon, sensitive to the interruptions it produces, a fitting symbol to the writing fringe as we're swept away by the immediate and drastic actions of plot, and characterization, with just a tinge of deception and intrigue added in for good measure.

I sip my tea and write the next chapter with him online; we share intimate sentiments between the pauses, personal reflections in the golden, late autumn afternoon. The emerging book surrounds us, protects us in a steadfast circle where we both roam free hand in hand, in a legendary way,

tranquil to the storms that seek our demise and immune to them. It's been a day of pursuit and small pleasures, an aimless stroll that has now found direction. We have secured our souls vigorously and with potential. My coffee cup is empty but my tea up, full. Tomorrow I get to drink the impulse of his voice,

it will be the first time I hear it since the collaboration. I close my eyes and I'm in the Cloisters, sidestepping the bicycles that are prone to flying up and down the narrow paths between the patches of sunlight. My hair is short, dark, and I'm chasing butterflies in the herb garden, before collapsing onto the cobblestones, fast asleep.

~

The morning tea smells of tension and burnt water. I often think about staggering into failure before the awareness of triumph. I see streaks of blue between the brief interludes. There was once a time when I walked with a confident gait but that ended quite a while ago.

I'm still a chameleon though,

and can adapt well to change, and to me, it's crucial for growth. I do
welcome the decent intervals of edgy silence; it 's a sign of intelligence,
of caution. I don't know why I fear his call so much; if the true nature of
an individual is in their work, then we've already been privy to one another's
souls and why not want a word, now, in private?

~

If one believes in all matters mundane, then why not all matters outside
of the norm? His voice is a safe house, there's a resting lull that carries
its way straight to my heart. Beneath the waves of inflection; the intonations,
stress, emphasis, beats, measures, rhythm, cadence, modulation
and accentuation, is an overturned boat,

one I understand completely and feel compelled to rescue. This is our first
real contact yet I feel like I've known him for ages, this old soul who now
forms the arc that blazes away brightly, symbolically, at sandy beaches,
where we exchange glances through the meters of time, captive within
the beauty of nature, with a hand over both our hearts.

~

The phone calls have escalated and become more intense. I think we're
at our highest level; we've become one another's life's blood. Hours
pass and we hardly notice; contemplation in the color of the moment,
only our moments are rich, wealthy, with the power of joy, and the
amazing fortune of discovery.

He moves me, incites my desires for everything I had never given a
second thought to before. We're well connected, influenced by
the growing love that makes no demands but just is; an extension of
our souls released for a few seconds at a time, to roam the cosmos,
a reminder of the gift we've both been given,

that should never be taken for granted. If I close my eyes, I feel
the drunken sense of elation. He's with me, and there is no distance,
no need for phone calls. The mornings pass to the afternoons, and
the afternoons to the nights under the cover of warm embrace, where
we go to sleep in one another's arms,

and wake up in one another's arms, enjoying the days hand by hand,
immune to light that shines directly into the open wounds of our
past, sterilizing and cauterizing as the healing takes place, the fragments
breaking away before becoming whole, in a deviation strictly
regulated by a low voice and the realization of unconditional love.

~

If I was ever rescued, he did it; he rescued me. I've always loved the
Cloisters; the top of the world is what I used to say as child hiking up
the path to the monastery; where wordless stone settings and steep
narrow stairs creaked silently through the metal wares all things modern.
The sun always seems to radiate more brightly there, even though,

there's a certain abandoned and dark feel to it, to the surroundings, until
you reach the top. Imbedded with bits and pieces of debris is fortitude,
strength, which has withstood the hands of time, of centuries. The gardens are
alive with recognition and love that fills long empty hours; and the
featureless clouds float down, comforting, endless.

I get to meet him there, for our first encounter. I get to walk that path with
him to the top of the world erasing my past with every step even as I
remember it. I get to look into his eyes touched by the backdrop of crystalline
air that warms with the brightness of his eyes, foretelling our future.
Together, we get to loop around the winding paths of moments, with no
control.

~

We've been with one another many times now, across the broad greens,
the busy intersections that keep us apart with physical distance, yet,
emotionally, mentally, intellectually, spiritually, he is never far away.
I know my love spins around him, protects him, guides him closer to me
as does his love for me.

His smile is a flash of pink in a hailstorm of rainbow colors that
bring joy, all familiar, all unbroken. I'm hopelessly in love, and
my love for him reigns in longevity, with endurance. He has made me a batch
of Vanilla Chai Tea, his own concoction. I drink, thinking of him, thinking the
blend needs a pinch of Damiana, just a pinch.

~

A pillow stuffed with star anise seeds, keeps away nightmares. There's
a passing moon shadow that delivers the edge for the right herbal
blend, commanding every spice to flow in the opposite direction,
where dormant hearts are awakened once again by the image and impulse
of tidal creeks and earthly visions.

Mars, Fire, Masculine, stirs the pot. The aromatic brew fogs up
my kitchen window. It's mother's recipe for an upset soul, one
of purity and innocence, boiled steadily by coiled burners, whose
gaze appears with the result of premonition; I am his forever his,
and he is my forever mine.

~

1 1/2 tsp Chai Rooibos
1/4 tsp Damiana
1/2 tsp Lemon Verbena
1/2 tsp of honey
1/2 cup fresh full cream milk
1/2 tsp. Catnip
Pinch of Cinnamon powder
Tiny pinch of Ginger
1/2 tsp fennel powder
1/2 tsp cardamom powder
1/4 teaspoon nutmeg
1 1/2 cups of water
Vanilla creamer

Chapter 2: He Says

"Excuse me..." I cleared my throat, my thoughts mysteriously lost amid the restaurant drone. My date smiled. Her eyes skipped from table to table to catch which pretty face caught my fancy this time. "The strangest thing just happened," I remarked, once again applying my fork to my meal -- something plain, something German -- except now the taste was as vibrant as a race car on my tongue, a blend of sweet and spice that traveled down and idled unsettlingly in my groin.

My date stared at me contemptuously as if I had left her out of a private joke, and for some reason I can't explain, I kept her waiting, savoring my secret with each delectable bite. The scrape and clatter of dishware fell in place of conversation as I searched though the food with tongue and taste bud looking for a woman's touch, and I almost found it, felt it vanish in the air.

My date asked the waiter for the check, hoping to intercede, but there was no going back. My wanderlust continued long after the date was spoiled, and the relationship that went with it. I search now in restaurant after restaurant, my hunger unabated, chasing after a phantom aroma the flavor of fire and earth and water and sky, a taste that left the imprint of its memory on the tender surface of my budding heart.

~

Mr. Lee's Tea Room. The entire establishment was the size of some department store windows. Teas of every texture and color, their subtle differences as vast and variable as an encyclopedia of love.

I found the place purely by accident, mistaking it for an antique shop, but once I had found it, I thought I would never leave. One small table and two chairs occupied the corner like an open invitation. I sat, body stiff, excited at the prospect of trying something new, something exotic, something I'd been searching for all my life.

A small Asian man approached with pad and pencil, a towel draped across his sleeve. He nodded his head as if I'd been a longtime customer. "Can you recommend --" The words had barely left my lips when he grunted. "Vanilla chai." He scribbled on the pad, tore off the sheet and slapped it on the table, making it wobble. Then he walked away.

Of all the obvious unknown surprises I could have chosen, I had settled for something familiar. Vanilla chai. A co-opted brand found in fast food chains and on grocery store shelves. Vanilla chai. How unoriginal, how un-exotic, I thought.

But the man was back in two minutes tops, delivering something rich and foamy in a mug too hot to hold. Its steaming aroma sent saliva spilling across my tongue. The smells of cinnamon, ginger, clove and cardamom spun in sensuous strands the untold story of my youth, as if contained within the flavors were answers to the greatest riddles known to man, and all one had to do was take a sip.

But as I raised the still blistering hot mug to my lips and drank, there was only one question on my mind and one motive in my heart--to resurrect the phantom I had glimpsed that day in that restaurant, to take her hand and make her real and get a taste of life at last. But instead I burned my mouth and dropped the cup, spilling every drop.

I could have sworn I heard the proprietor laugh, mocking my sad attempt at capturing a life I was willing to try but wasn't ready to have. I paid for my mistake just the same and left Mr. Lee's Tea Room wiser but still wanting.

~

I lay in bed, staring out my window, bathed in
moonlight. I feel her next to me; taste her on my
tongue. I can almost touch her but my fingers
fall through the pale blue luminescence, like
placing my hand in a waterfall only to watch it
come out dry.

I realize the reality that is she is as ethereal as
these thoughts, these fleeting images, these
imaginary flights. I can only hope that by putting
them into words, it will somehow make her real,
and one day we will be together, like this, side by
side, bathed in the luminescence of lost love now
found, bathed in the forever after glow of happiness,
bathed in moonlight.

~

Cross-legged, writing, cooking meals, making tea
with homemade recipes. I tried to find Mr. Lee's
Tea Room again but couldn't remember the route
I had taken, and the Internet was no help. My
kitchen cabinet now smells like cinnamon and a
host of other spices. I have green tea soap in my
shower. A constellation of scented candles light
the darkness I feel sometimes alone here in my
house; a darkness that feels like a half-sleep,
where the candlelight, the needle prick scents, the
taunt of her memory -- which isn't a memory but
a glimpse, a tease of what could be -- appears to
be guiding me toward the hour of my awakening.

~

Being alone wasn't the worst thing; being alone
in the company of the one I supposedly loved
was. Which begged the question: was I ever truly

in love?

I can't explain why this notion -- this woman of
my dreams -- is more powerful than what is real.
I only know that what was real was but a shell,
a hollow, empty existence that provided little joy
and no promise.

This is why I must find her. But how?

I had tried restaurants and tea shops, but they only
mimicked what I already knew, what I had already
tasted. I needed something physical, something
tangible, something that would let me know my
time wasn't wasted and my path was true.

~

Once again in my half-sleep I felt a nudge,
a sudden tickle on my chin, and awoke to
find a stray cat with white, white whiskers
on my bed. I stared at it, not knowing how
it got there or to whom it belonged. I had
never seen the cat before. But it knew me.

When the cat heard footsteps in the hall, it
leapt from my bed to my desk, walked across
the keyboard of my computer, the monitor
crackling to life. At last, the cat jumped down
and left the room. Seconds later, I heard my
landlord shout, "Damn strays!" Then a door
slam woke me.

The stray cat with the white, white whiskers
had been nothing but a dream. Why then did
I still feel the damp nuzzle of its whiskers
against my chin? Why, when I looked, was
the monitor on my computer now awake?

Now that I was awake, I got up, got dressed
and left my empty house in search of strays.

~

It's hard. To move beyond a past that gave little joy but provided the comfort of routine. It's hard. To hold a phantom lover in my arms, to taste her kiss, to make plans for a future that has yet to take shape. It's hard. To find comfort with the in between, like sleeping in a bed half made, like walking with one shoe on, one shoe off. It's hard. But while hard may not be bliss, it is far from unhappy. Hard is the distance I have traveled, and the distance I have yet to conquer. It's hard. But she makes the trip worthwhile.

~

The Internet is a world unto itself, a cosmic pipeline filled with the traffic of lost and lonely souls. Some are searching for attention, others for notoriety. Some search like prospectors for that next great vein of gold; and still others enter through the gateway, wearing their hearts on their fingertips, in search of the ultimate connection: love. As ethereal as love is, it's only natural that the Internet has become the world's largest dating service.

Instead of visiting restaurants and tea shops and chasing after phantom cats sent by phantom lovers, I joined several message boards for writers, to keep my mind active while my heart vacationed in limbo. I read the poetry I found there and even posted my own -- deeply personal expressions, things I wouldn't share with family members but felt perfectly comfortable laying bare for total strangers to see. Like shaking hands with people through holes in a wall, the Internet provides a layer of anonymity, a buffer that allows us to explore while at the same time protects us from risk. Here is where I found her.

Like the Devil or God, she had many names. She was a fractured spirit, and yet I knew who she was. She tried hard not to be found. But, like the ancient philosophers encrypting the keys to their knowledge, perhaps there was a certain code I had to decipher in order to unlock the secret that was her. Like a recipe for Vanilla Chai tea, all I needed to do was take each fractured piece and put them all in one cup, add water, and it would be magic.

I read her poetry, her stories, her musings. I saw her words, but I also felt the movement of her mouth and tongue. I felt the whisper of her breath, the tremble of her voice, the sweet harmonic intonation of her heart. The similarity of thought and desire was enough to make me weep, make me mourn for what I'd been missing all my life. All of this and I had yet to formally introduce myself.

~

Day by day, week by week, we get to know each other; through bits and pieces, comments and conversations. She's Cuban-Spanish; I'm German-Irish-English. She's a teacher; I'm forever a student. We talk of dream vacations, dream homes, a dream life where everything is peaceful, serene; where we are not alone. We talk of the one person we want to share this dream universe with.

And soon we realize our wants and hopes and wishes are so similar, so complimentary, we finally stop circling the question we've been avoiding all this time: How about each other? "I can be that someone," I tell her. And though she's afraid to open her heart one more time, expose it to the hurt she knows so well, she takes me up on my offer.

And so we begin, even though we began when we met in that restaurant, her phantom teasing my palette with a taste of what the future could hold.

And though she is now just words on a computer screen and a voice on the phone, which at times feels as much a figment of my imagination as her phantom was before, she is no illusion; no figure conjured from tea kettle steam. She is real.

And soon we will meet again.

~

Emotional affairs never end well. There is the prerequisite attraction, followed by a period of flirtation, followed by a sincere attempt to transcend the ordinary, the mundane. These affairs become all-too-serious all-too-quickly and like a turn-of-the-century experimental aircraft it flies momentarily but falls apart under the weight of its design.

I hasten to say our affair was different. Through past experience, we both knew what we were getting into. We constructed it well. We took our time. We didn't over-reach or throw caution to the wind. We were smart. We were patient. Because we knew what we had. And what we had scared us both. What we had was about to change our lives forever. All we needed was the courage to fly.

~

It's silly. She has rules. We don't meet in person for a year. If we're still together, then we'll meet. She's done this before. More than once. Each time it ended with disaster. She wants to be sure. I agree. Why not? What's the rush? What's the hurry? If it's meant to be, it's meant to be. Like a

recipe for vanilla chai tea. One needs the proper
measure, the right ingredients. Too much or too
little and the taste is spoiled.

I enjoy her online company, her words, her
intelligence, her quirks and craziness. She makes
me laugh, even when she doesn't mean to. Most
of all I enjoy her passion. Her energy. She loves
life, even though life has not been kind to her. She
has faith in people, even though many people have
let her down. She believes whole-heartedly in love,
even though love has done cruel things to her heart.
I know this because her path is my path, her road
is my road.

We feel connected in a way that transcends all
logic and reason. Words like destiny and twin flame
and soul mate are used to try and explain what we
have. And the fact that we haven't met makes it all
seem special, rare, magical. Should we risk peeking
behind the curtain? Should we risk offending the
spirits that have brought us together by foolishly
rushing into each other's arms?

We decide to wait, even though the desire to meet, to
complete this last leg of this long, long journey, tugs
at us daily. We will wait until the time is right. Until
it becomes something born not out of desperation or
loneliness or horniness or even curiosity, but something
altogether new. Something pure. Something natural.
The way we always thought it should be, but never
thought it would be for us.

~

Now that I know she's real, I dream about
her nightly. Our conversations continue
long after our waking hours. We embrace,
we kiss, we make love. It is as real as any
physical relationship, perhaps more-so,
because there is no one else but us, no other

world but the world of our own making.

I once believed that make believe was just an illusion, a safe haven from the all-too-harsh and painful reality of being. Like trinkets, I thought things like hopes and dreams and wishes were just shiny objects. Like gold at the bottom of the ocean floor I could never reach. Like stars in the night sky I could never travel to.

But I now know there are two realities--two ingredients--that combine to make what is truly real. Both look and feel and taste like reality, but put both together and the world awakens.

Perhaps this closeness I feel to her are these two realities converging, getting closer with each passing hour, moving the way the moon sometimes moves to intercept the sun, creating a momentary burst of darkness and light, a super reality that eclipses all else.

Perhaps I am the moon to her sun and our paths are, and have always been, destined to cross.

~

I tell her she's the reason I was able to open my heart. She tells me I must have opened it myself. How else could I have found her?

Like the gentle swirling motion of a cup of tea releasing its fragrance, there needed to be an action, a movement on my part, a stirring from somewhere down deep that allowed my heart to open in such a way as to transmit a signal--to release a soulful fragrance--that only another heart as peculiar as mine could detect. Of course hers would have had to do the same.

This is why I am in awe and constantly asking myself how can things like this--like us--happen? How can the combination of two entirely different ingredients create something so powerful and pure and completely unique? How can things such as distance and time and place have so little meaning? How, if not by magic?

~

We dream of traveling the world. She wants to go to Cuba, her family's homeland. And though I've never been to an island country I can envision myself there. I can feel my feet in the ocean water, the warm air on my face. I can hear the breeze. It's all very real to me, as if we will be there at some point and I'm just seeing it from a distance.

Ever since I've met her it's been like that. It's as if we are both finally in the life stream that we are intended to be in. And this stream, this path, lends us the ability to see into our future, feel, hear, touch the edges of our dreams-- which aren't dreams at all but future realities. Such is the power of love.

And this love I have for her is like no other. It feels like it comes from somewhere that isn't entirely within me. It is as if our union has drawn love and light from all around us, and like a solar wind these collective energies are gently propelling us on our way toward our eventual destination.

Perhaps we have it all wrong. Perhaps the world travels within us, pushing us to places we are meant to be, toward people we are meant to be with. Perhaps all that is needed is for us to open ourselves up, take everything in, and allow the world to be our guide.

~

It has been three months since we confessed our love. Now, a year seems like an eternity. She forgoes her one-year rule and we set a date to meet. Almost immediately the questions surface, the doubt seeps in. What if we've created a love that can only hang suspended like some ethereal mist, like an aroma that we can taste but when we reach out cannot feel? What if when we meet eye-to-eye, face-to-face, we recoil from what we see because the flesh and blood reality doesn't match the ideal our imaginations have shaped for us? What if when we touch there is no spark, no ignition, no heat that burns like the flame that lights our yearning? It is then we realize that all our presumed risks and all our imaginary flights are nothing compared to the danger of bringing our secret, silent world into being. It could all come crashing down around us like a dropped cup of tea too hot to hold, where the taste is better savored from afar. What if fear devours us before we even give our future a try?

~

As writers we believe in fantasy. As romantics we believe in love. Love that can walk between worlds. Between the here and now and the there and then. Our time is without second hands. Our hearts beat to the rhythm of the earth. Our spirits soar in the rarefied air of the sky. Our love shines like the sun, and our passion rises like a full moon in the night. If we are deceiving ourselves then we would rather live uninformed than to acknowledge that deceit. We would rather die with love in our hearts then live with the pain of never having accepted it. If it is illusion then we are master magicians, master liars, master thieves. But as writers we also believe in truth, and truth strips fantasy down and lays it

bare. In truth we are in love, in body and in soul,
in our spirit and in our bones, forever and always,
in love.

~

The taste of her
lingers,
like the bite
of cinnamon
after a cup
of vanilla chai tea--
a cup made of flesh
yielding
to the pressure
of my tongue,
a spice
too elusive
to describe.
Again and again
I drank,
savoring
its unique flavor,
my tongue entreating--
just a tip,
as if too hot,
then plunging in
with abandon,
my lips clinging
to the outer rim.
Unlike a real cup
this one took
what I gave,
then gave back
ten fold,
my thirst for it
just as
bottomless.

~

I touch her skin,
so soft, so smooth
like Napoleon cream;
hills and mounds,
plateaus and valleys,
each unique spot
a moving, shifting
landscape beneath
my fingertips, my
tongue, my lips;
so sweet the fragrance
of her love, her
sweat like nectar
squeezed from heart
ripened vines entwined
with mine;
no threshold too great,
no depth too deep
to plumb, we press,
we mesh, we merge
flesh with flesh,
we purge our palates
for just one taste
of something special,
something pure,
something undeniable,
we try…
and yet each time
it slips through our
fingers, escapes our
tongues, but leaves
a residue behind
just tangible enough
to tease our senses
into thinking
next time will be
ours.

~

And though our physical touch

contains the chemical spark, it is
our eye-to-eye communication
- the shape of our language, the
weight of our words, the vibratory
nature of our voices - that contains
its essence. Our love is not in the
making but in its intent. Our love
is not in the culmination but in its
creation. Our love is not only a
product of this moment, this reality;
it is a product of all moments, all
realities embraced and enraptured
into one.

Chapter 3: They Say~One Voice

As I stare into a cup of hot tea,
I see the liquid whip
around savagely for several
minutes after stirring.

The cream razors, swells, until
it lapses into a long silence,
naked of any course or apparent
fate, like a late night walk

along the edges of a lake, where
wind driven pools break in shimmers
that crest hard against slippery stained
rocks shaped by moonlight.

A moonlight that knows our names
and predicts our fate but in its silence
leaves us forever guessing
which direction we should turn,

like the cream that swirls
and curls, affected by forces beyond
mere temperature and volume
but a need to reach an equilibrium

that will satisfy both the tea
and the cream. Meanwhile, the spoon
sits idly by, unseen, not unlike
the invisible hand of God.

~

I walk through the hallways of his home,
his mind calls me, points me to where
memories are spent and love is made; a
few minutes of daylight left, I look at my
watch, he doesn't wear one, even though
I've given him one. It's poetic,

beautiful in how it all works. Time is innocent,
not held hostage or threatening. I close my
eyes, spinning clockwise, drawing magickal
energy into our essence, he the cup, glowing
brightly, I the tea, drawing in life while still
inside him.

~

I can see the lake from my window. She
hasn't been here, hasn't seen it for herself.
She lives over a hundred miles away but it
might as well be a thousand. She says time
stretches, as well as distances, everything
is fluid, I can be her eyes.

As instructed, I make a cup of tea. I whisper
words of clarity into the steam rising from its
lip. I inhale its spicy fragrance not once, not
twice, but three times. On the third time my
senses begin to vibrate with her presence. I
feel displaced. I feel her within me.

~

We lapse into silence; it's a comfortable
component that meets no resistance, having
slept in eternity, tangled to intervals of light
rain that make drowsy love to us both as we
disappear inside one another, summoned at
short notice to relive this night, as one.

~

Faint traces of vanilla in the air,
upon recipes of such a note that
awaken the lungs to something
strangely comforting. He's at
my door again, this man who rules
my heart, this man with gray temples

whose face exposes the purity of his
soul.

We trip over shackles shed, our
surrounding skin, soft, freckled,
slightly reddened. His eyes are
almond, browned: Cain sugar, once
abandoned and dark, featureless to
white walls. He's hunger under my
breath, passion reserved just for me,
in need, want and bound oath.

In our wild wilderness we atone for
our sins, watch the herbs grow outside
the fence of life cold to the touch.
Fire burns brightly in the hearth that
brews awakened vitality tea as we make
love, much of our world uprooted by
the gota kola, ginseng, peppermint,
rosemary, eucalyptus, black tea base,

and just a hint of damiana.

~

Together we move along independent
pathways that happen to be the same;
our wants, our wills both coincidental
and complimentary; never an unopened
door, an unanswered question, never
a conceit.

In her dark eyes I see the fathomless
depths of possibility; in her smile I
feel the joys of our collective memory
both past and future; on her lips I
taste the sweet and spice of resolution
and forgiveness;

and when we touch our chemistry
ignites, our twin recipes combine to

prove both combustive and compulsive;
we become addicts to the liberating
pleasure brewing just beneath the
surface of our skins; and all that has

yet to be discovered.

~

Vanilla Chai Tea with a hint of Damiana
contains the lifeblood of our souls. Beneath
the herbs are the templates that regulate our
destiny. We wonder about this arrangement
in our attempt to understand why. We fight
to remain conscious, realistic, with every
sensation that builds, responding to our
love, reminding us the cavalry is well on its
way and found inside our hearts. We have the
power to save one another, if we can only let
go of fear.

I drink; smile, anticipating the tasseomancy.
In my divination I see a pure-bristle shaving
bush and stainless steel chrome-plated blade.
I smell the old scent of Dominica Bay Rum
from ages past and realize he is the equivalent
to an immortal soul, an immortal soul that
has always been linked to mine. I hesitate,
knowing I tend to shoot gentlemen like him
from twenty paces; but his eyes are all the
ammunition I need to surrender. There is no
mention of ransom or negotiation. I am freely his.

~

Compared to her I'm a brute, raw in my
emotions, unpracticed in the skills of true
love, uncomfortable with being loved in
return. But she is patient. When I'm with
her time bends, past present future, it's all
the same. There is no hurry, no rush to

love, to please, to make right. Mostly I
am patient with myself.

I had no idea love could be this simple. If I
had I would have been miserable, searching
for it night and day in an attempt to find
perfection. I realize now love cannot be
found, now matter how hard you look for it;
it will allow you to see it only when you are
ready, only when the brilliance of its light
can be appreciated, not blinding; only when
the path it illuminates is true.

~

He says I'm magick, yet he's the one who mixes
a special blend of sensual oils, regulated by his
love and want for me. His brown eyes play mind
games with the long empty hours I spend away from
him, but the oils provide a spiritual mecca, a safe
haven that feeds my desires with the aroma of
almond extract and sweat.

With his touch he whispers my name, sees me, as
I really am, vulnerable. The blue bottle of oil lights
up the air around us warms in the palms of his hands.
Together we tense up, relax, and moan, as our bodies
peel away at the different layers. It's not about sex, but
emotional wholeness. With each breath he takes my sighs
into his hands, my heart a pound of raw meat;

he has the power to really hurt me if he wanted to. I
stare at the flames of our passion as they fall away
from us, he, still holding me in his arms. His smile
strengthens our bond, the way silence touches the soul
in those moments when you just want to crawl up
into a ball and disappear. My lungs breathe out my
contentment. In his surrender, I am cleansed.

~

We put aside the remaining cheese and crackers;
several grapes sit uneaten. The TV drones. She makes
me a cup of tea and we sit, always face to face, like
two children awakening from a long dead sleep, our
bodies always touching, connecting in ways that are
not meant to be sexual but tend to lead us in that
direction.

Into the kitchen, where I press against her, kissing
her neck as she performs mundane chores. She turns
into my arms and our kisses export us to a casita in
Cuba, the sound of nearby ocean surf pounding in
concert with the breeze like twin heartbeats filling
the silent measures each one provides.

We move then into her bedroom where the sun greets
us, warming our already heated skin. We peel away
the layers, not stopping when our clothes are removed.
We're explorers now, mapping both outer and inner
landscapes, our progress both enhanced and eased by
the scented oils I bring.

We lie unbound on a sensual oasis, the two of us
the only souls to inhabit the paradise we've created.
The scent of orange and spice accompanies the ocean
breeze. The taste of salt and sweet cinnamon clings
to our lips. We savor these quiet eternities as time
slides from view like a setting sun.

~

He wears Hugo Boss cologne. I ask him to.
The scent reminds me of a fiery sunset on
the Cuban coastline. I feel his energy, his
hands on my breasts; even with my eyes
squeezed shut I see him start to bloom, swell,
like a soul waiting to be housed by a body.

He seems stronger, more sure of who he is.
I bite my lip, slip into the den of his sin in
response to his touch. He explores me, slowly,

flirting with my anticipation. My bed rests
under an open window; summer, spring, winter,
fall, my window is always wide open.

You'd think it would be an introduction to chaos,
but for me it serves to restore balance in my life.
I look up and watch the planes fly overhead,
envisioning stealing away to exotic places with
him, where the sands are warm, even when rain
pounds down on them.

~

She wears makeup unfailingly. She tries to cover up
the flaws she thinks everyone can see. But there are
no flaws, only what's real. I tell her she's beautiful and
she looks away, as if searching for evidence to prove
I'm wrong. But I know what's true. I know when I look
into her eyes the make-up is merely protection, a thin
layer of courage she does not need.

Soon the heat we generate dissolves this layer, resolves
this issue. She caresses my arms and shoulders, feels the
strength I possess. She allows me to see her in full daylight,
naked as the sun. I am encouraged to do the same, to let
go, relax, be as naked as she. And in our moment of lustful
abandon, she knows with an unspoken certainty that she is
courageous, she is protected, and she is loved.

~

We're lost, somewhere on Gunhill Road
in the Bronx. He drives, holding my hand
with reassurance. I say I'm scared, nothing
looks familiar, but as my lips part, I moist
them with excitement. Getting lost with him,
means more time with him. He laughs at my
floating sense of direction; and I can't read a
map to save my life.

~

We're lost; again, driving along roads with
names that mean little to her and even less
to me. But still we're laughing. Maybe love
means finding the joy in being lost together.
It's funny how she can read thoughts and
pick up emotions out of the air, but when
it comes to side streets and boulevards, she
has not a clue.

~

There are days that are intended to mean
something. A fine breeze moves off the
leaves, frosting car windows with a white
film of silence. It is the beginning of winter;
the beginning of morning smells filled with
a combination of earthly and spiritual aromas,
both natural and man-made.

I wake to sleep in his arms, taking his essence
into my very being just to keep him close
beside me. I feed my fate with his destiny,
as sunlit brush tumbles with a fantasy of
animated colors. Cinnamon lingers in my
teacup, draws sugar back into my mouth.
He tightens his embrace around me,

promising sandal-scented brews of steaming
sweetness. His voice can be a wellspring of
beauty, to its foundation where dreams come
true. The pace of our love is fast, airborne, like
the planes we now watch together from my
bedroom window. Many search and find nothing,
I searched and found him. I consider myself,

one of the lucky ones.

~

The seasons have shadowed us. With autumn came

the baring of our truths, the gradual stripping of our
souls. No secrets, the mantra, like a cleansing wind,
from the very beginning.

Now that winter is here we stand naked, our inhibitions
lost, our innocence regained, crystalline and pure. Love
blankets everything and everyone around us. We are
accepting, we are open.

Come spring we'll know how the trees feel, arms spread
wide, hands in the air; we'll be uplifted as the ground swells
and bursts beneath our feet; and the breath in our lungs will
be fresh and warm again.

And after that, our lives will be nothing but one long
endless summer.

~

The color white usually covers
featureless walls, but when snow
falls and settles on the bough of
trees, it's a recipe for awakening
that is strangely comforting, like
a white note, slipped subtly beneath
a door, or the creak of a metal door,
opening just a tad, enough to seize
the forces of nature, little bits at a
time.

Today is such a day, subtle. Breakfast
began with some Vanilla Chai Tea,
bottled water, and a few pieces of
chocolate. The smell of pine trees
is still settled inside my nose from the
previous day, when vendors lined busy
streets cashing in on the Christmas
excitement. Trees die for this? I didn't
want a tree, not this year. But today is
one of those subtle days,

where you remember certain things that
wedge themselves into your soul. One
of the best Christmases I ever had was
when my sister, her roommate, Roberta
and I cut down our own pine in a
Connecticut tree farm. Snow was falling,
not aggressively, but in slow motion,
those large flakes that seem to float on
into eternity before hitting down and
melting.

I scrutinized the snow, how it fell without
any form of hesitation or evidence of
struggle. In the night's distance, flashlights
from other tree cutters outlined the barks
of individual trees. I followed some footprints
to an opening where a medium sized pine stood,
and said, "This one!" Only a couple of hacks
and it was mine, with no evidence of a real
struggle. I looked up, catching snowflakes
with my tongue as they kissed my face,

and I remembered the story, Snowflakes Only
Melt, They Never Die. Crouching down I
probed the snow settled on the ground with my
bare hands to what lay beneath the surface. Earth!
Alive! Regenerative! Snow is beautiful, a good omen,
like the subtle brushstrokes on a blank canvas. And
Christmas, the true meaning beneath the surface,
has a beautiful subtlety all its own. This year, I
do want a Christmas tree, not a real one, because
memories like mine should be protected, put away,
preserved, but a tree nonetheless, a white one,
already decorated and abandoned in some store

front waiting to be rescued. After all, I like
the subtlety of that symbolism. When he comes
today we will get our tree. When he comes today
I will tell him all about this and he'll give me that
quizzical frown that I so love that is uniquely his.
When he comes today, we will be absorbed into a

joyous street-scape like two child-like spirits
floating through the amazing wonder of it all,
totally innocent, fortunes spent, elbows touching,
in a journey of subtle silence.

~

There's a halfhearted drizzle today, dark
and raw, yet the music it makes is magickal.
Last night a blue jay sang outside my bedroom
window, all night long. He often comes,
accompanied by an adventurous squirrel I've
named, Nuts. They are an unlikely pair those
two, and its strange to think how they met,
becoming partners in crime.

If I could bottle them up and keep them in a
large clear wish jar, I would. I like the purpose
of their routine, how they monitor one another's
proceedings with useful love and intelligence. In
a way they are already preserved behind glass,
in a jar made of wishes occupied by objects
of that symbolism. Sometimes I wonder if I'm
the squirrel and he the blue jay; life our wish jar.

~

"Let's write a book," she says, "to document our
love." I think, what better way to tell our children
how mommy and daddy met, how they fell in love,
how they nurtured that love and made it something
greater than themselves, how that love grew into
the spiritual and physical home it is now, how love
can be a testament, love can conquer all obstacles,
love can make even the most far reaching dreams
reality, how words like soul mate and twin flame
are not just made up ideals only found in fairy tales,
how the sun seems brighter, the sky bluer, how the
taste of vanilla chai tea is much more flavorful when
made with love. "Okay," I say, and I make more tea,
a cup for her, a cup for me, and we get to work.

~

He retraces the steps of his childhood,
the fire where he lost a microscope,
his way of analyzing, of operational
surveillance.

I trace mine back to my beloved
childhood home on Arden Street,
where a fire from the furniture store
beneath the art deco building,

took away my symbolic microscope
to the world around me. Nestled on
the top floor, apartment 6c was my
safe way of monitoring the world,

from a distance. I liked being the
outsider looking in. From my bedroom
window I could see the shower spray
of Fort Tyrone Park,

the one I loved to play in, that always
gave me a sort throat and fever afterwards.
I could see the pinnacle of The Cloisters,
the place my father loved,

and the place my mom took me to
everyday. I remember the path to The Cloisters
becoming routine, I remember taking
it for granted.

The blame for that lies with me; it was
an oversight on my part. Even though I
could see everything from my tower on
the sixth floor, I was blind,

to what really mattered. I was blind to
the beauty and magick of moments, freely
given and freely accepted. Moments, like

a gust of wind that pellets water

into our faces.

~

She shows me her world one fragment
at a time. Sometimes it's a photograph,
sometimes a building we drive by on our
way to her sister's apartment, sometimes
it's a memory jogged by something that
was said.

Though the course of her life has been
different than mine, the similarity of our
experiences are striking, as if we've been
shaped and steered by forces beyond our
understanding.

If it hadn't been for us writing about our
personal experiences and having the courage
to post them for all the world to see, we
would have never read each other's words
and felt in them a kinship.

If we each hadn't been at a point in our life
where we felt it was necessary to set out to
heal the damage done to our wounded spirit,
we would have never been open enough, or
vulnerable enough, to allow each other in.

And the fact that we live only a hundred miles
apart - close enough to see each other on a regular
basis and yet far enough to keep the process of
getting to know each other slow and incremental
- was both coincidental and a blessing.

Little did we know, the moments we used to
cherish when we were growing up - moments
that served as solitary comfort - would one day
find the ear that was meant to hear them, and

the heart to appreciate their necessity.

~

We have our good days
and our not so good,
but our days are never bad,
because any day together is a blessing.

Is this love? is not a question
but a search for answers
along an infinite landscape
where the architecture of our dreams exists.

If we had not opened our eyes,
we would have not seen each other
and recognized the near-catastrophic
betrayal of our individual beauty.

We have our good days
and our not so good,
but any day together has been
and will forever be a welcome imperfection.

~

I ruined a batch of tea this morning;
my heart just wasn't in it. I've never
understood people who see the world
as either black or white, a one-word
answer-yes or no. Life is broken up
into so many possible outcomes it's
scary, and sometimes screams echo
over landscapes as fingernails claw
over the earth, torturing the day with
the incoming threat of a night's death.

I almost want to give up, to run into
a cloudburst and jut the knife forcing
the rain to come so it can dissipate,
passing quickly. I feel like split wood,

stay there, do the right thing, go here
and be happy. Sometimes words hold
little conviction and a call for action
is needed as a way of fighting for one's
own true joy and love. The truth is, he
is my joy and my love. So with a little

bit of Bluebell for luck and truth, I make
a new batch of tea. We have our good days
and our bad days, among the aromatic
vapors of magick that shadow the wilds
of dusk with the promise of a runaway
moonlight; we have our good days and
our bad days of beautiful imperfection,
among the flames that heat the herbs,
whispering our names in the pot, like a fatal
song of love made strong by two unwavering

hearts.

~

Our love was the flame that lit the burner that
heated the water for our tea. And like a flame
it was unpredictable. It was attractive and yet
dangerous.

There were days when that flame was blue,
and we held it in our hands the way we held
each other, fueled with intensity and tenderness.
And it was beautiful.

And then were days the flame sputtered and
we could not move for fear of blowing it out,
when even a cup of tea could not provide
enough warmth.

And in between the sputtering and the beauty
there was heat and passion that threatened to
consume us if we were not cautious, careful,
but most of all courageous.

And now we stand comfortably side-by-side,
in love, twin flames burning brightly, like two
separate entities birthed from the same sacred
source.

~

Love is the most powerful force in the universe...

~It is magick~

www.ingramcontent.com/pod-product-compliance
Lightning Source LLC
Chambersburg PA
CBHW071752020426
42331CB00008B/2283